Bats

Written by Rachael Davis

Collins

This is a bat.

It has thin wings.

Bats can hang and nap.

bat mum with a pup

If the sun is up, bats will nap.

This bat naps in a bat box.

bat box

Bats can nap in thin gaps, as well.

The sun has set.

Bats will zip off to get bugs.

Is this a bat?

Yes!

No. This is a rat!

Yes!

Set up a bat box

Bash it.

Fix it.

Hang it.

Check it.

13

Bats!

15

Review: After reading

Use your assessment from hearing the children read to choose any GPCs, words or tricky words that need additional practice.

Read 1: Decoding
- Turn to pages 2 and 3. Ask the children to read the words. Then ask them to identify the words with the digraph "th". (**this, thin, with**)
- Ask the children to read the word **hang** on page 3. Discuss its meaning in the context of what the bat does. Say: The bat hangs onto the branches with its feet. It hangs upside down.
- Ask the children to read page 4. Encourage them to blend in their heads silently (if they need to) before reading aloud.

Read 2: Prosody
- Model reading with prosody. After you have read, ask the children to have a go. Use the suggestions below.
  - On page 8, read clearly, emphasising the words that show it is the end of the day. (**sun**, **set**)
  - On page 9, emphasise the words that give the most important information. (**zip off**, **bugs**)

Read 3: Comprehension
- Talk about the facts included in the book. Ask: Which pages did you find the most interesting? What makes bats different to lots of other creatures? Do you think the author likes bats? Why?
- Use the pictures on pages 14 and 15 to model how to recap the content of the book. Ask the children to have a go. Ask: What are bats' wings like? (*thin*) What can bats do well? (e.g. *hang on well*)
- Bonus content: Encourage the children to follow the lines from the photos on page 10 to the answers on page 11. Ask: Did any of the answers surprise you? In what way?
- Bonus content: Turn to pages 12 and 13. Talk about the process of making a bat box. Can the children describe what happens at each step?